NEW YORK

THE CITY AT A GLANCE

120 Wall Street
This ziggurat designed by Buchm
occupies an entire block in the r
financial district. Completed in 1
structure is a fine example of art deco.

Woolworth Building
A pre-WWI embellishment to the New York
skyline, Cass Gilbert's pile earned National
Historic Landmark status in 1966.
See p015

One WTC
The tallest tower in the western hemisphere
(with spire), One WTC's height is 1,776 feet, the
year of the US Declaration of Independence.
A viewing deck on level 100 opened in 2015.
See p009

8 Spruce Street
Frank Gehry's 2011 skyscraper has a wave-like
facade and was, briefly, the highest residential
building in NYC at 265m, soon pipped by One57
(see p072) and 423 Park Avenue (see p014).

Brooklyn Bridge
Fly into JFK Airport and no doubt this is how
you'll cross the East River to arrive downtown.
It was designed by John Augustus Roebling,
who died before its completion in 1883.

Manhattan Bridge
Ralph Modjeski and Leon Moisseiff's 1909
bridge now carries seven lanes of traffic
and four subway tracks. It has undergone
$920m of reconstruction work since 1982.

Empire State Building
Architect William Lamb's high-rise (King Kong's
favourite) opened in 1931, and the views from
the 86th-floor observatory are fabulous.
350 Fifth Avenue, T 212 736 3100

INTRODUCTION
THE CHANGING FACE OF THE URBAN SCENE

Why do we love New York? Perhaps it's that incomparable skyline, or the city's irrepressible spirit. Or the fact that it can challenge even the most cosmopolitan urbanite – if you can't do it here, you probably can't do it anywhere. Gotham is a tough act to top.

In the period following the tragedy of the Twin Towers, New York has gradually regained its enthusiasm for the new. Architects have been reshaping the cityscape, particularly in the southern tip of Manhattan and north of 34th Street. Creative industries have sprung up in support of homegrown talent and trades; American design, in particular, is being celebrated. The glitz and glamour are still there, but originality and sustainability are now valued just as highly. The prevalence of retailers selling handcrafted or artisanal goods, and restaurants focused on farm-to-table, even roof-to-table, shows that New Yorkers expect something authentic for their buck. Recently, the emphasis has shifted further towards the customised experience – personalised hotel minibars, tailor-made jeans, digital gallery tours and diner-generated tasting menus.

Artists and hipsters are still migrating to the outer boroughs, to Brooklyn and, increasingly, Queens, but now that districts such as Williamsburg and Park Slope are as expensive – and as elitist – as Tribeca or Chelsea, the less well-trodden areas are the more viable options for setting up home or a business. Formerly on the fringes, these neighbourhoods are fast becoming the epicentres of cool.

ESSENTIAL INFO

FACTS, FIGURES AND USEFUL ADDRESSES

TOURIST OFFICE
Third floor, 810 Seventh Avenue
T 212 484 1200
www.nycgo.com

TRANSPORT
Airport transfer to Manhattan
AirTrains run 24 hours to the subway and
Long Island Rail Road, which links to Penn
Station. The journey takes 50 minutes
www.panynj.gov/airports/jfk-airtrain.html
Car hire
Avis
T 212 593 8396
Car service
Dial 7 Car & Limousine Service
T 212 777 7777
MetroCard
A seven-day metro and bus pass is $57.25
www.mta.info/metrocard
Subway
Trains run 24 hours a day, every day
www.mta.info
Yellow cabs
T 212 639 9675
(T 311 for enquiries such as lost property)

EMERGENCY SERVICES
Emergencies
T 911
Police (non-emergency)
T 311
24-hour pharmacy
CVS
630 Lexington Avenue
T 917 369 8688

CONSULATES
British Consulate-General
845 Third Avenue
T 212 745 0200
www.gov.uk/government/world/usa

POSTAL SERVICES
Post office
90 Church Street
T 1 800 275 8777
Shipping
UPS
T 212 680 3118

BOOKS
**Block by Block: Jane Jacobs and
the Future of New York**
(Princeton Architectural Press)
Here is New York by EB White
(Little Bookroom)
Long Island Modernism 1930-1980
by Caroline Rob Zaleski (WW Norton & Co)

WEBSITES
Architecture/Design
www.cooperhewitt.org
Newspaper
www.nytimes.com

EVENTS
Frieze Art Fair
www.friezenewyork.com
ICFF
www.icff.com
NYCxDESIGN
nycxdesign.com

COST OF LIVING
Taxi from JFK Airport to Manhattan
$60
Cappuccino
$3.50
Packet of cigarettes
$12
Daily newspaper
$2.50
Bottle of champagne
$65

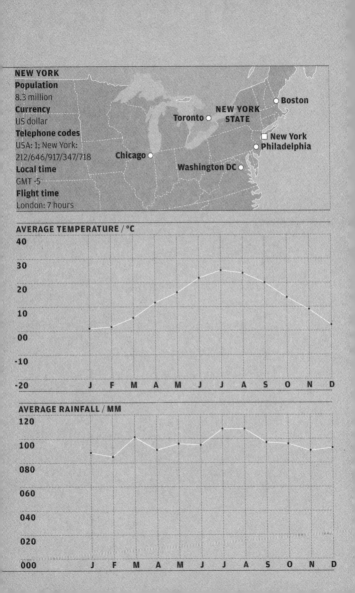

NEW YORK

Population
8.3 million

Currency
US dollar

Telephone codes
USA: 1; New York:
212/646/917/347/718

Local time
GMT -5

Flight time
London: 7 hours

Toronto
NEW YORK STATE
Boston
Chicago
New York
Philadelphia
Washington DC

AVERAGE TEMPERATURE / °C

40
30
20
10
00
-10
-20

J F M A M J J A S O N D

AVERAGE RAINFALL / MM

120
100
080
060
040
020
000

J F M A M J J A S O N D

NEIGHBOURHOODS

THE AREAS YOU NEED TO KNOW AND WHY

To help you navigate the city, we've chosen the most interesting districts (see below and the map inside the back cover) and colour-coded our featured venues, according to their location; those venues that are outside these areas are not coloured.

TRIBECA/THE BATTERY

Manhattan's south tip could not be more diverse. Downtown's most compelling area, Ground Zero (see p010), is taking shape and nearing completion 15 years after 9/11. Tribeca is a younger version of Soho, full of design studios (see p082), as well as an impressive new tower of its own (see p072).

UPPER WEST SIDE

Archetypal liberal intellectual territory, this residential district attracts money old and new – its vast apartment blocks are like cruise ships steaming across the island. Its cultural focal point is the Lincoln Center (70 Lincoln Center Plaza, T 212 875 5000), a superb ensemble of 1960s modernism.

WEST VILLAGE

Darling of both indie and luxury brands (especially along Bleecker Street), the leafy West Village has a vibrant yet intimate ambience. Here, Manhattan assumes a human scale, with cosy neighbourhood eateries, 19th-century townhouses and pretty streets, such as Perry and Charles.

SOHO

Once an artists' quarter, where cast-iron industrial buildings were turned into lofts and studios, the mood is now more Kenzo than De Kooning, and Soho can feel very touristy. However, it does have great shops such as The Apartment (see p026), Proenza Schouler (see p084) and Alexander Wang (see p094), and good galleries (see p028).

UPPER EAST SIDE

This is quintessential rich-bitch territory, where liveried doormen help social X-rays carry bag upon bag after a day's shopping on Madison. It's home to a trio of venerable museums: the Cooper Hewitt (see p068), the Guggenheim (1071 Fifth Avenue, T 212 423 3500) and the Met (see p072).

MIDTOWN

NYC's central business district includes Times Square – the backdrop for the bright lights of Broadway or a tacky neon-lit tourist hell, depending on your take. Highlights include the view from The Roof at the Viceroy hotel (see p016) and the slick Aldo Sohm Wine Bar (see p052).

CHELSEA

The must-see draw in Chelsea is the hyper-hyped High Line (see p030). It's perhaps more fascinating to walk the streets due to the sheer volume of heavyweight art galleries (see p056). Venues like Toro (see p046) have restored a hipness that gentrification had diminished.

EAST VILLAGE/LOWER EAST SIDE

Traditionally a working-class immigrant area, the Lower East Side is still a cultural melting pot, and home to some of NYC's edgier art spaces and bars, as well as SANAA's New Museum (see p073). To the north, the East Village has been heading upmarket since the 1980s, while Noho draws fashionistas to its many boutiques.

LANDMARKS

THE SHAPE OF THE CITY SKYLINE

How can you pick out a landmark building in a city that possibly contains more instantly recognisable skyscrapers than any other? Perhaps owing to its relative youth, New York has never been shy about making a statement with modern architecture. Thanks to the affluence of its citizens, the Big Apple has been able to call on the talents of almost every architect of note over the past century to create its incomparable skyline. And with the 2015 addition of 432 Park Avenue (see p014), the tallest residential tower in the western hemisphere at 426m, the city shows no sign of sleeping.

The restoration of downtown continues and, following the 2014 opening of Davis Brody Bond's subterranean National September 11 Memorial Museum (Liberty Street, T 212 312 8800), accessed via Snøhetta's pavilion, the World Trade Center site is taking shape, with the completion of Santiago Calatrava's winged transport hub. At its heart is an emotionally charged plaza (overleaf), where two huge waterfalls occupy the footprints of the Twin Towers. Rearing above are SOM's 541m One WTC (285 Fulton Street) and Fumihiko Maki's quietly impressive 298m 4 WTC (Greenwich Street).

We understand if you want to escape all the building. Central Park, Frederick Law Olmsted and Calvert Vaux's 341-hectare oasis, is perhaps New York's most symbolic landmark for its impressive absence of construction. Take time out under a 150-year-old oak. *For full addresses, see Resources.*

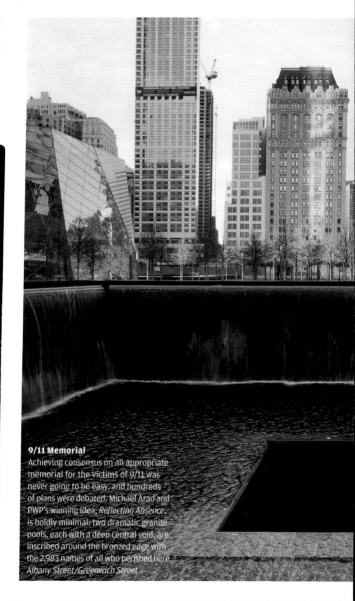

9/11 Memorial

Achieving consensus on an appropriate memorial for the victims of 9/11 was never going to be easy, and hundreds of plans were debated. Michael Arad and PWP's winning idea, *Reflecting Absence*, is boldly minimal: two dramatic granite pools, each with a deep central void, are inscribed around the bronzed edge with the 2,983 names of all who perished here.
Albany Street/Greenwich Street

AT&T Building

This gargantuan 1932 art deco structure, which was designed by American architect Ralph Walker, was originally known as the AT&T Long Distance Building; it housed the telecommunications giant's transatlantic offices and equipment. In the 1990s, AT&T made this its headquarters, although the firm has since sold up. Its brick-clad bulk (all 106,838 sq m of it) is quintessentially Gotham-like in form, and the lobby boasts the obligatory tiled map of the world on one wall. The building may not be among the city's best-known landmarks, nor even Walker's finest work (this is usually said to be the erstwhile Irving Trust Company HQ that's located at 1 Wall Street). However, from its profile to the materials used, the AT&T could not be found anywhere except New York, and for that it is a masterwork.
32 Sixth Avenue

Hearst Tower

Fresh from remodelling London's skyline with 30 St Mary Axe (the Gherkin), Norman Foster tackled the HQ of the Hearst media empire. The diamond-faceted facade of this 46-storey tower, completed in 2006, thrusts out of an existing art deco building that was commissioned in the 1920s by the newspaper mogul William Randolph Hearst; the six-storey structure was always intended to form the base of a landmark high-rise. The new blends seamlessly with the old, thanks to the dramatic lobby that extends up through the lower floors and provides access to the rest of the building. And it's not just a pretty sight. The tower is environmentally friendly too – it was constructed with 90 per cent recycled steel and consumes roughly 25 per cent less energy than its neighbours.

300 W 57th Street

432 Park Avenue

The elongated, slender and seemingly impossibly tall form of 432 Park Avenue has led to comparisons with a matchstick. New York's second highest building after One WTC (see p009) is perhaps difficult to like; the 37,160 sq m of real estate in 'Billionaires' Belt' is parcelled into just 104 condos for the global super-rich (its website is in seven languages, the second being Russian). Yet Rafael Viñoly's strict geometry – 84 square storeys, each with six square windows per face – has earned it a begrudging respect. Amenities such as a golf training centre, restaurant, pool and spa, not to mention the views (west to the Hudson, south to Brooklyn, north to Central Park and the Bronx) might make the $95m price tag on the penthouse more palatable, although it is often shrouded in cloud.

432 Park Avenue, www.432parkavenue.com

Woolworth Building

For some 17 years after its opening in 1913, Cass Gilbert's Woolworth Building was the tallest in the world. His client, five-and-dime-store magnate Frank W Woolworth, was wealthy enough to pay the $13.5m bill in cash. This, coupled with the structure's gothic proportions, earned it the moniker 'the cathedral of commerce'. Even today, its sheer scale is awe-inspiring: it stands at 241.4m high, and there's room for 14,000 office workers across 60 storeys, all of which are served by 34 elevators. The top 30 floors are being converted into flats. In the spectacular lobby, which is lined with marble and lavishly decorated with bronze and mosaics, there are medieval-style gargoyles, including caricatures of Gilbert and Woolworth, guided tours lasting from 30 to 90 minutes can be booked online. *233 Broadway, www.woolworthtours.com*

HOTELS

WHERE TO STAY AND WHICH ROOMS TO BOOK

The boutique hotel scene is resurgent, and gone are the days when staying in Midtown meant skipping the style. It continues to draw, as evidenced by Roman and Williams' Viceroy (120 W 57th Street, T 212 830 8000) and the towering Park Hyatt (153 W 57th Street, T 646 774 1234), while the eco-luxury 1 Hotel Central Park (1414 Sixth Avenue, T 212 703 2001) has staked its claim. This prompted the establishment to up its game – the Loews Regency (540 Park Avenue, T 212 759 4100) underwent a $100m makeover in 2014.

NoMad (north of Madison Square) is the latest haunt of hotelier Ian Schrager, who has partnered with Marriott to launch the chic Edition (5 Madison Avenue, T 212 413 4200) in the iconic 1909 Met Life Tower, modelled on the Venice Campanile and recognised for its four clocks. It champions a home-away-from-home vibe also evident at the welcoming Sixty Soho (opposite) and The Ludlow (180 Ludlow Street, T 212 432 1818), where the oak panelling and mosaic floors pay tribute to the heritage of the Lower East Side.

There are attractive options on the West Side too. A few blocks from the Hudson, Hotel Hugo (525 Greenwich Street, T 212 608 4848) mixes industrial elements with glossy finishes and vertical gardens. And in Chelsea, The High Line Hotel (180 Tenth Avenue, T 212 929 3888) – it was only a matter of time – in the 1865 red-brick General Theological Seminary cuts a dash amid all the galleries. *For full addresses and room rates, see Resources.*

Sixty Soho

Quite the scene when it opened in 2001 as 60 Thompson, the hotel was given a multi-million dollar renovation a decade later to become the flagship of Jason Pomeranc's Sixty brand. It still has destination public spaces – the posh Gordon Bar, 'coastal' Italian restaurant Sessanta, a sexy lobby (above) with nooks for tête-à-têtes and a roof with breathtaking views. Pomeranc's art collection – including commissioned work by Harland Miller – adds personality. The 97 rooms and suites are drenched in light through huge windows that offset the dark wood, deep velvet and timber floors. Studded pillows by Alexander McQueen top beds, while the novels on shelves, and art and photography books strewn across side tables accentuate the 'you live here' ethos. *60 Thompson Street, T 877 431 0400, www.sixtyhotels.com*

Paper Factory

The outer boroughs continue to be fertile ground for hotel openings, encouraged by the success of the Wythe (see p020). Now, in of-the-moment Long Island City, comes this $27m overhaul of an 8,000 sq m – you guessed it – paper factory near Kaufman Arts District. Toy cars, Buddha statues, an iconic red UK phone booth and repurposed industrial appliances fill the common areas and lobby (above), which also features an iron staircase that spirals around a rainbow of hardback books. The kitsch might be a little overwhelming for some, but the 123 rooms, including suites and a penthouse, are among the city's most affordable. The polished concrete, hammered metal doors and exposed pipes are offset by works of contemporary art and sleek lighting.
37-06 36th Street, T 718 392 7200, www.paperfactoryhotel.com

The Marlton

Hotelier Sean MacPherson once described this luxe bijou hotel as 'Honey, I shrunk the Ritz'. Nestled in the heart of Greenwich Village, the former college dorm has been transformed into a nine-storey tribute to Parisian chic. Sculpted mouldings and Serge Mouille-style ceiling lamps bedeck the petite but light-filled rooms, such as the Queen Deluxe (above), and the lobby features patterned carpets, dark wood panelling and reupholstered sofas. The hotel also houses an elegant brasserie, Margaux (T 212 321 0111), a haunt of the local fashion set; Bellocq tea and Ferndell coffee can be ordered from the Espresso Bar. It's all a stylish, polished counterpoint to the urban-industrial aesthetic that has proliferated across town in recent years.
*5 W 8th Street, T 212 321 0100,
www.marltonhotel.com*

Wythe Hotel
Opened in 2012, the Wythe has given
Brooklyn the grown-up hotel it deserves.
The factory building has been wisely
preserved, and the decor of reclaimed
pine furniture and bespoke wallpaper
(King Room, pictured) is the right foil,
softening the industrial edge. Dine at
Reynard (T 718 460 8004), then drink
in the Manhattan skyline from the bar.
80 Wythe Avenue, T 718 460 8000

Archer

In the heart of the garment district, the Archer is a well-priced option in Midtown's burgeoning portfolio. It riffs on the area's heritage; an industrial quality is captured through red brick and black steel. The tone is set from the lobby's Bugatti Bar and the David Burke restaurant Fabrick (T 212 302 3838), where dyed fabric 'dries' from high ceilings. The 180 rooms are spread over 22 floors. You won't be swinging many cats in the standards; the higher-up corner rooms are more spacious and have wood floors. There are various considered local touches: millwork from Queens, upholstery from Westchester and turndown cupcakes from Baked by Melissa, but the highlight is the sceney rooftop bar Spyglass (above; T 212 730 0538), directly facing the Empire State. *45 W 38th Street, T 212 719 4100, www.archerhotel.com/new-york*

The Marmara Park Avenue

The Istanbul brand's 21-storey flagship has, as you might expect, a Bisazza mosaic-tiled subterranean pool and a proper hammam. However, local artist Joe Ginsberg and his team have custom-made almost everything else in the rest of the hotel, from the bar's handblown glass to the steel vestibule that greets you. In rooms, black-and-gold Mylar wallpaper replicates Ginsberg's photos of the Third Avenue Bridge (which Marmara's owners helped finance) while hardwood floors, neutral velvets, leathers and Jim Thompson silks add texture (One Bedroom Suite, above), and fully equipped kitchens in some suites make these fine Manhattan pied-à-terres. The 40 highest rooms have killer terraces. Check out (if you can bring yourself to) on the in-room iPad Air.
114 E 32nd Street, T 212 427 3100, park.marmaranyc.com

24 HOURS

SEE THE BEST OF THE CITY IN JUST ONE DAY

You'll never want for things to do in New York. What with all the eating, drinking and shopping, it can be hard to find time for other pursuits, so our recommended plan of attack is to hone in on the cultural highlights of just a few neighbourhoods.

The best way to see the city is on foot, and our itinerary focuses on lower Manhattan. First, grab a coffee at Ninth Street Espresso (75 Ninth Avenue), inside the Chelsea Market, before touring the district's many galleries (opposite). From here, make a beeline for Soho for a dose of retail heaven (see p026) and to refuel on Italian-inspired dishes such as octopus saltimbocca at the buzzy Charlie Bird (5 King Street, T 212 235 7133). Ease post-lunch lethargy by following a stroll through the cobbled streets with a nose around Donald Judd's studio (see p029) before looping back to Chelsea to visit the High Line (see p030) and the Whitney (see p074).

For dinner, head to the East Village and the scene-making bistro Dirty French (180 Ludlow Street, T 212 254 3000) in the hip Ludlow hotel (see p016) or the refined Tuome (536 E 5th Street, T 646 833 7811), where the fusion of US ingredients and Asian flavours is a hit. Have a nightcap nearby in unmarked speakeasy Attaboy (134 Eldridge Street) or, indeed, Nitecap (120 Rivington Street, T 212 466 3361) from the Death + Company (433 E 6th Street, T 212 388 0882) team. All three have super lists of knockout bespoke cocktails. *For full addresses, see Resources.*

10.00 David Zwirner

Representing more than 40 artists, such as Yayoi Kusama, Doug Wheeler and Dan Flavin, and eight artists' estates, David Zwirner now has two galleries in Chelsea. The 19th Street location (T 212 727 2070) occupies three single-storey units that were once garages and stables, while the newer 20th Street gallery (above), opened in 2013, is a LEED-certified new-build by Selldorf Architects. The industrial edge of the exposed concrete facade is tempered by teak window frames and panelling at the entrance. There are two exhibition areas, including a 465 sq m column-free space. While you're in the area, also check out Hauser & Wirth (T 212 790 3900) and the Gagosian spaces on 21st Street (T 212 741 1717) and 24th Street (T 212 741 1111). *537 W 20th Street, T 212 517 8677, www.davidzwirner.com*

12.00 The Apartment by The Line
Opened by uber-stylists Vanessa Traina
and Morgan Wendelborn (who has since
departed), The Apartment is an inviting
concept store and physical iteration of
the online fashion and lifestyle portal
The Line. The showroom is a light-filled
Soho loft divided into rooms, each one
offering a vision of modern living, thanks
in part to the set design by Carl Sprague,
a Wes Anderson collaborator. On display
are wares spanning the apparel, beauty
and design realms, featuring items from
industry stalwarts including ME SkinLab,
Protagonist, Mansur Gavriel and Rodin,
alongside Jean Prouvé chairs and other
vintage curios sourced locally. The studio
is open on Wednesdays and Saturdays
from about midday, and during the rest
of the week by appointment only.
3rd floor, 76 Greene Street,
T 646 678 4908, www.theline.com

14.00 101 Spring Street

Providing a brilliant insight into the life and work of Donald Judd, this former Soho textile factory, which the artist bought in 1968 and turned into a live/work space, is now a rich celebration of his philosophies on art and architecture. Restored by Judd himself, 101 Spring Street was taken under the wing of the National Trust for Historic Preservation after his death in 1994. A juxtaposition of industrial 19th-century fixtures and Judd's abstract works, the five-storey space also displays furniture and art that Judd collected on his travels or from his peers – other seminal artists of the 20th century, such as Dan Flavin. To gain access, visitors must book one of three daily 90-minute guided tours. It's closed Monday, Wednesday and Sunday. *101 Spring Street, T 212 219 2747, www.juddfoundation.org*

16.00 High Line

A strip of elevated parkway by the river in Chelsea has been the regeneration project on everyone's lips for the past few years. This disused 1930s freight rail track was threatened with demolition in the 1990s, prompting two local residents, Robert Hammond and Joshua David, to form a not-for-profit group, Friends of the High Line, to save it. The result, designed by Diller Scofidio + Renfro, as well as James Corner Field Operations, is a truly inspired public space, which is used from dawn to dusk. The first section, Gansevoort Street to W 20th Street, opened in 2009, and a second stretch, to W 30th Street, in 2011. The latest phase, the High Line at the Rail Yards, now runs up to W 34th Street, and wraps around the ongoing construction of Hudson Yards (see p072).
T 212 206 9922, www.thehighline.org

20.00 Eleven Madison Park

Chef Daniel Humm's three-Michelin-starred masterpiece is still *the* quintessential NYC culinary experience. Located within the landmark art deco Metropolitan Life North Building, the high-ceilinged dining room, designed by Bentel & Bentel, is both grand and intimate; clubby leather banquettes are matched with ornate inlaid wood and gold-leaf ceiling. The multiple-course tasting menu is priced steep at $225, but few leave disappointed. The emphasis is on local ingredients and seasonality: in the summer, Montauk fluke might make an appearance; in spring, North Fork ramps; in the fall/winter, Hudson Valley apples and squash. If you don't feel like splurging on the whole three-hour experience, snag a table at the front bar for the à la carte. *11 Madison Avenue, T 212 889 0905, www.elevenmadisonpark.com*

URBAN LIFE
CAFÉS, RESTAURANTS, BARS AND NIGHTCLUBS

Despite the hectic pace of life, eating and drinking out are sacred to New Yorkers, and the diversity of the scene is the city's great forte. Tasting menus are increasingly popular – bow to the chefs' ingenuity at Alder (see p036), Contra (138 Orchard Street, T 212 466 4633) and the gorgeous Almanac (28 Seventh Avenue S, T 212 255 1795). Other treasured stalwarts are experimenting with new ventures, such as Via Carota (51 Grove Street), a no-reservations Italian-inspired hit by Jody Williams and Rita Sodi, or expanding existing ones, like herbivore haven Dirt Candy (see p040). Semilla (160 Havemeyer Street, T 718 782 3474) is 'vegetable-forward' too, but with a Latin touch. Also full of invention, modern Mexican is taking off at The Black Ant (60 Second Avenue, T 212 598 0300), while Enrique Olvera rewrites the rules altogether at Cosme (see p042). As for Asian cuisine, Uncle Boons (7 Spring Street, T 646 370 6650) takes a leftfield approach to Thai and hipster fave Mission Chinese Food (171 E Broadway) has grown up and moved digs.

Although the enthusiasm for flamboyant clubbing here might have waned, there are numerous intimate spots like Up & Down (see p038), or plead with your contacts for the password to Zazou (179 MacDougal Street) in Greenwich. The party is still pumping in Brooklyn, at the hip Bossa Nova Civic Club (1271 Myrtle Avenue, T 718 443 1271) and neon-lit warehouse Output (74 Wythe Avenue). *For full addresses, see Resources.*

Russ & Daughters Cafe

Beloved Jewish stalwart Russ & Daughters, which has been through four generations since 1914, celebrated its centenary by opening this full-service outpost on the Lower East Side. Smoked fish aficionados can now take a seat for their supper, and order an egg cream (milk, soda water and vanilla or chocolate syrup) or bloody Mary from the newly minted cocktail bar. It is modelled on the original Houston Street venue. Lightbox signs announce *rugelach*, *bialys* and *schmaltz* herring; there are boxes of *matzoh* and jars of *halvah*; and sturgeon and salmon take pride of place. A 1950s-style counter anchors the white-tiled space and booths are decorated with family portraits. In 2015 a branch opened in The Jewish Museum (T 212 423 3200). *127 Orchard Street, T 212 475 4881, www.russanddaughterscafe.com*

WHIT...
TIAMO...

STANDINO...

VIN D'AGUILA
9 26 40
FAÏENZA TREBBIANO
9 27 44
TRUTH OR CONSEQUENCES CHARD
8 26 48
KARAVITAKIS
THE LITTLE PRINCE
7 23 38
CHANNING DAUGHTERS TOCAI
9 27 50

RED

LA COUX ROUGE 8 25 45
SAN FELICIS RIOJA
9 27 50
AGRICULTURA TINTO
8 25 45
EMPIRE BUILDER CAB FRANC
9 27 50
CHANNING DAUGHTERS
SCULPTURE GARDEN
13 36 65
EL REDE MALBEC
9 27 50
GRAN PASSIONE
9 30 58
ZWEIGELT

...SERVICE

ROSE
WIEMER
9 22 40
CIDER
SOVEREIGN
7
BEER
BALLAST POINT SCULPIN IPA
4 7

Lois

Manhattan's first all-draft wine bar, Lois opened in Alphabet City in late 2014. There are 16 rotating labels served from the keg, detailed on a triangular letterboard behind the bar, as well as two beers, and a paired menu of small plates ranging from rillettes to cheeseboards and charcuterie. It's an enjoyable way to educate your taste buds without breaking the bank — glasses range from $4 to $11. The sleek space also takes the pretension out of the process. Michael J Groth, in collaboration with artist Robert Ogden, has installed warm woods such as white oak and mahogany, brass-accented pendant lights, sconces and chandeliers, a banquette upholstered in vintage Turkish kilim and an unfinished-tin-tiled ceiling. Lois opens at 5pm (4pm on weekends).

98 Avenue C (Loisaida Avenue),
T 212 475 1400, www.loisbarnyc.com

Alder

Still generating a buzz, Alder is helmed by the molecular gastronomy pioneer Wylie Dufresne, who has created a multi-course tasting menu of whimsically deconstructed classics. The interior design by Jennifer Carpenter matches the inventive mood of the cooking: a textured brick wall is offset by a ceiling of salvaged fencing, hung at varying angles to create a ripple effect.
157 Second Avenue, T 212 539 1900

Up & Down

Richie Akiva and Scott Sartiano of 1 OAK and Butter have turned the former celeb hangout, the Darby supper club, into this bi-level nightspot. The Up part (above) is styled after an Italian villa, with leather banquettes, antique mirrors and palm trees. Below is where all the action takes place, down a mirrored staircase with a light installation activated by body heat. It is decorated with art by Tracey Emin and designer Roy Nachum, and has various secret spaces – a karaoke room behind a bookshelf and a hidden photobooth. Early on, it's all very convivial around the pool table but as soon as the DJ gets going, the dancefloor livens up. The impromptu live performances by the cream of hip hop and R&B have become the stuff of legend. *244 W 14th Street, T 212 242 4411, www.uadnyc.com*

Momofuku Ko

David Chang revolutionised the NYC food landscape a decade ago, bringing high-end dishes at affordable prices to downtown spaces. Ko, the jewel in the Momofuku empire, got a reboot with a move just off Bowery and an expansive tasting menu ($175) where the culinary process in the open kitchen remains an intrinsic part of the experience. Watch as creations such as sea urchin with chickpea *hozon* purée or razor clams with pineapple *dashi* and basil are prepared and served on Brooklyn ceramicist Wynne Noble's plates and Mud Australia's Limoges porcelain. Graffiti and multimedia work by US-Korean artist David Choe are showcased throughout, and the entryway features pieces by US-Taiwanese painter James Jean. Reservations must be made online, up to 15 days in advance.
8 Extra Place, www.momofuku.com

Dirt Candy

Chef Amanda Cohen's vegetarian pioneer traded in its original 18 seats for 60 at this Lower East Side location that attempts to evoke 'the overgrown charm of a garden peeking through the cracks in a concrete sidewalk'. Partially designed by Cohen, with Turett Collaborative Architects, the restaurant is also something of a homage to Cecil Beaton's Ascot scene in *My Fair Lady*, through its monochrome colour scheme, and details such as the flower murals on the whitewashed brick walls by graffiti artist Noah McDonough. Try the jalapeño hush puppies, signature broccoli dogs and decadent curried paneer fries. Dirt Candy not only has a brilliant name, but also a no-tipping policy – one of only a few restaurants in New York to have one. *86 Allen Street, T 212 228 7732, www.dirtcandynyc.com*

Tørst

Since its 2013 launch, Tørst has taken the pairing of food and craft beer to another level, and that's all down to the skills and imagination of the venue's owners, Daniel Burns (ex-Noma and Momofuku) and Jeppe Jarnit-Bjergsø (Evil Twin brewery). An alternating selection of 21 beers is available on tap, and there are more than 200 bottles to choose from; we kicked off with an Evil Twin and a Tørst exclusive from the Swedish brewery Omnipollo. The bar snacks have a Danish slant (rye bread, smoked trout, cured meats) and the Scandi theme extends to the interiors. Brooklyn's Haslegrave brothers accented the space with a combination of woods and marble. If the beer-drinking works up your appetite, try Luksus, adjoined to the bar

615 Manhattan Avenue, T 718 389 6034, www.torstnyc.com

Cosme

Chef of the acclaimed restaurant Pujol in Mexico City, Enrique Olvera's sultry Gramercy space is a dark den of culinary pleasure that can seat 140 yet delivers a deeply intimate experience. Order three dishes each to share, perhaps the duck *carnitas*, *chicharrón* (pork crackling) with radish, and *uni tostadas*, paired with a fiery agave cocktail from the buzzy bar.
35 E 21st Street, T 212 913 9659

Pearl & Ash

Chef Richard Kuo oversees the tiny kitchen at the dinner-only Pearl & Ash, serving up small plates with big flavours from around the world. At the bar, sommelier Patrick Cappiello has compiled one of the city's most interesting wine lists (it stretches to 81 pages) and Eben Klemm's cocktails, also designed to complement the food, are similarly inventive – try a Black Betty with Byrrh, blackberry and lavender. Brooklyn's Sway Design Collective conceived the interiors, installing poplar tables and an eye-catching wall of box shelving, filled with moss and ephemera. Hovering just between Noho and the East Village, it is located below boutique hostel The Bowery House (T 212 837 2373). Next door is spin-off French eatery Rebelle (T 917 639 3880). *220 Bowery, T 212 837 2370, www.pearlandash.com*

Narcissa

Inside The Standard East Village (T 212 475 5700), Narcissa has won quite a following since launch in 2014. The restaurant uses produce that is grown on André Balazs' farm, Locusts-on-Hudson, and has built a strong reputation for its rotisserie cooking and a West Coast approach to flavours and ingredients. Chef John Fraser, who is also responsible for Upper West Side's Dovetail (T 212 362 3800), applies the method to meat and poultry, in dishes such as baby chicken with spiced sausage, charred eggplant, fava beans and pine nuts; and vegetables, like crisped beets with bulgur salad and apples. The dining room has a cool, Nordic-Shaker appearance, with blondwood accents and a mural by Andrew Kuo, and there's an expansive terrace too. *25 Cooper Square, T 212 228 3344, www.narcissarestaurant.com*

Toro

Housed within a former Nabisco factory facing the Hudson river, Toro is a laidback affair serving traditional and new-wave Barcelona-style tapas and *pintxos*. The wood and exposed-brick interiors draw on the industrial origins, and large windows allow the light to stream in. Launched by chefs Jamie Bissonnette and Ken Oringer, who partnered up with Doug Jacob and Will Malnati, as a Big Apple counterpart to their respected Boston restaurant, Toro seats 120 diners. We suggest you grab a stool at the *plancha* bar to watch as dishes such as grilled corn with espelette, aioli, lime and aged cheese, or roasted bone marrow with beef-cheek marmalade are whipped up. Wash them all down with the sangria, made using seasonal ingredients. *85 Tenth Avenue, T 212 691 2360, www.toro-nyc.com*

Chefs Club

Following its success in Aspen, Chefs Club arrived in the Puck Building, a Romanesque revival pile named after sculptor Henry Baerer's gilded imps. Culinary director Didier Elena and executive chef Matthew Aita replicate the dishes of some of the country's best talents, who come to guest cook in short stints in the intimate 16-seat 'studio'. Expect a hearty seasonal menu, with plenty of meat, game and seafood and earthy garnishes. Within the brick vaults, the open kitchen is naturally the focal point of the masculine space, which features walnut wood, marble, concrete, leather, brass and steel, with tableware by Uhuru from Brooklyn. The art installations by Murray Moss in giant suspended vitrines include a huge Himalayan salt deposit.
275 Mulberry Street, T 212 941 1100, www.chefsclub.com/new-york

All'onda
Contributing to the recent renaissance of Greenwich Village, All'onda takes a fresh look at Venetian fare. Chef Chris Jaeckle has added Japanese influences to his interpretation of *cicchetti*, from black truffle arancini and chicken liver crostini to crudo, risotto and pasta. The mix of brick, tiles, wood and metallic details is the work of Silvia Zofio and Jack Dakin. *22 E 13th Street, T 212 231 2236*

Antica Pesa

The first outpost of the renowned Roman restaurant, opened in 1922, serves *cucina rustica* in refined surroundings, bringing a refreshing urbanity to Williamsburg and its dining scene. The interior designers, Brooklyn-based BArC Studio, have created three distinct zones: the front area (above) caters for larger groups; the middle section has a marble bar and cosy lounge with a fireplace; and through the rear is the main dining room, decorated with walnut wood, white walls and pendant lights. Order one or two of the pastas, which are excellent. *Schiaffoni all'amatriciana* (with cured pork jowl, crushed tomatoes and pecorino) and the spaghetti *cacio e pepe* (with parmesan, pecorino and black pepper) are brilliantly executed versions of the classics.
115 Berry Street, T 347 763 2635, www.anticapesa.com

The NoMad Bar

Chef Daniel Humm and restaurateur Will Guidara are growing their empire, after Eleven Madison Park (see p031) and the stylish NoMad Hotel (T 212 796 1500). The independent NoMad Bar showcases Leo Robitschek's bespoke cocktail offering in a soaring room with clubby leather booths and highball tables surrounding a dramatic backlit mahogany bar. Designers Stonehill & Taylor have drawn on the district's high-

low aesthetic through Mackenzie Rollins' photos (Louboutins on a dirty street, etc) and the work of local artisans – trays from Brooklyn's Worth Manufacturing, uniforms by Kimmie Kakes and dinnerware by Jono Pandolfi. Try the extravagant gin-soaked Forbidden Dance, and soak it up with the chicken pot pie with truffle and foie gras.
10 W 28th Street, T 347 472 5660,
www.thenomadhotel.com

Aldo Sohm Wine Bar

Sommelier Aldo Sohm opened this venture over the way from the Midtown restaurant Le Bernardin (T 212 554 1515) where he has advanced wine pairing to an artform. Designers Bentel & Bentel have managed to emulate the feel of a wealthy friend's expertly decorated living room. The rear (above) is occupied by an oak bar that doubles as a communal tasting table, and high tables surround a massive, U-shaped Donghia couch. Colourful artworks by Sir Terry Frost and Catman hang alongside shelves of eclectic personal effects. If you are feeling peckish, there are cheese and charcuterie platters, light salads and a decadent truffled pasta. More excitingly, at 10pm each night, a small-batch or rare vintage is opened and offered by the glass. *151 W 51st Street, T 212 554 1143, www.aldosohmwinebar.com*

The Cecil

The Hotel Cecil was a Harlem flophouse for jazz greats like Billie Holiday, Miles Davis and Thelonious Monk, who was discovered at the adjacent Minton's Playhouse (T 212 243 2222), before it caught fire in 1974. Forty years on it has been resurrected as a dark, sexy Afro-Asian-American restaurant (and social housing), designed by Sarah Garcia in collaboration with Splice and run by chef Alexander Smalls and his protégé Joseph 'JJ' Johnson. Chaz Guest's ink- and oil-on-linen paintings hang on wallpaper flecked with Masai warriors, and there is a mesh sculpture of an entwined couple behind the bar. Order the sublime gumbo, coconut grits (a southern US staple similar to polenta) and oxtail dumplings before catching a gig at the restored Minton's. *210 W 118th Street, T 212 866 1262, www.thececilharlem.com*

INSIDER'S GUIDE

NADIA SARWAR, PHOTOGRAPHER AND BLOGGER

Born in England, Nadia Sarwar moved to the States in 2011 and now has a live/work studio in Bushwick (www.nadiasarwar.com). 'New York is a hotbed of inspiration,' she says. 'Everyone is so in love with their city – the energy and positivity is palpable.'

She starts the day in Williamsburg with a Scuttlebutt sandwich from Saltie (378 Metropolitan Avenue, T 718 387 4777) and a cereal milkshake from Momofuku's Milk Bar (382 Metropolitan Avenue, T 347 577 9504) to take to Grand Ferry Park to savour the views. Sarwar likes to drop by the 'wonderfully curated' About Glamour (107a N 3rd Street, T 718 599 3044) to peruse the rails of vintage fashion before lunch at either 983 (983 Flushing Avenue, T 718 386 1133) – 'the Caesar salad is unparalleled' – or Little Mo (1158 Myrtle Avenue, T 929 210 8100), where she orders the *bao*.

In Manhattan, Sarwar will often make a beeline for Miss Lily's (132 W Houston Street, T 646 588 5375) to get a taste of Jamaica, Kuma Inn (113 Ludlow Street, T 212 353 8866), a hidden Asian tapas joint, or Cha Chan Tang (45 Mott Street, T 212 577 2888), which serves Hong Kong-style dishes. In her home borough, she enthuses about the tasting menu at Mexican restaurant Xixa (241 S 4th Street, T 718 388 8860). However, she will usually end up at the 'atmospheric' Hotel Delmano (82 Berry Street, T 718 387 1945) in Williamsburg. 'There's an extensive menu and delicious drinks.' *For full addresses, see Resources.*

ART AND DESIGN
GALLERIES, STUDIOS AND PUBLIC SPACES

An influx of international wealth has all but banished the memory of the recent recession, driving the launch of galleries, studios and fairs to create an art market that is more frenzied than ever. The relocation of the Whitney (see p074) has boosted the pre-eminence of Chelsea, which is home to some 350 ventures, while many others are located in Tribeca (see p064). Even Soho, long since deserted by working artists, remains a rich source of design (see p063).

And the frontiers continue to expand with the colonising of new arts districts in other areas and boroughs. Exhibition spaces have sprung up on the Lower East Side (see p066), near the venerable Studio Museum in Harlem (see p061), and in Long Island City (see p065) and Sunnyside in Queens. In Brooklyn, they are adding to the character of Bushwick, Sunset Park and Red Hook (see p058). Even the subway connecting these neighbourhoods is fertile ground for public art, thanks to the popular MTA programme (see p060).

Meanwhile, the city's cultural pillars tend to their empires. The Met (see p072) now inhabits the Whitney's old home, the Cooper Hewitt (see p068) has undergone a massive modernisation, and MoMA (11 W 53rd Street, T 212 708 9400) and the Frick Collection (1 E 70th Street, T 212 288 0700) are both looking to expand. As the *New York Times* aptly put it: 'There is no New York art world. There are only art worlds – a planetary system with no sun at its centre.' *For full addresses, see Resources.*

Chamber

Founded in 2014 by Argentine Juan Garcia Mosqueda, this design boutique displays experimental and unusual furniture and objects, and limited-edition artwork. In a vaulted gallery in a Neil Denari building that abuts the High Line, Mosqueda invites prominent figures to curate collections in two-year cycles. The inaugural group of 100 items is presented by Job Smeets and Nynke Tynagel of Antwerp atelier Studio Job, and includes original work by Tom Dixon, Wim Crouwel, Alessandro Mendini, Piet Hein Eek ('Waste Waste 80 x 80' chair, above left) and Richard Hutten ('New York Thing' chair/table, above right), as well as new talent from the Low Countries. A little bizarrely, a bespoke perfume accompanies each venture. Closed Sunday and Monday.
515 W 23rd Street, T 212 206 0236,
www.chambernyc.com

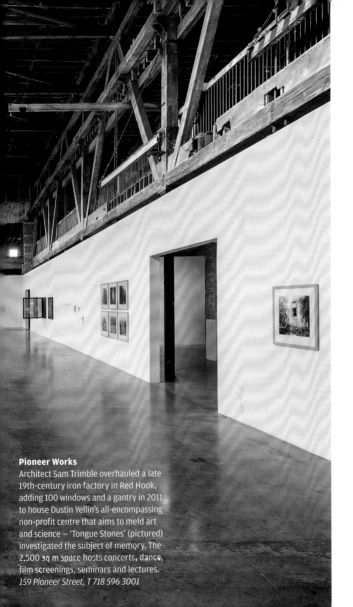

Pioneer Works
Architect Sam Trimble overhauled a late
19th-century iron factory in Red Hook,
adding 100 windows and a gantry in 2011
to house Dustin Yellin's all-encompassing
non-profit centre that aims to meld art
and science – 'Tongue Stones' (pictured)
investigated the subject of memory. The
2,500 sq m space hosts concerts, dance,
film screenings, seminars and lectures.
159 Pioneer Street, T 718 596 3001

MTA Arts & Design

The Metropolitan Transport Authority's (MTA) ongoing underground art collection now comprises more than 300 works that decorate subway stations throughout the five boroughs. Launched in the 1980s to rehabilitate a grubby public transit system with subterranean mosaics and sculpture, the initiative has expanded to encompass a variety of media and formats, including musical performances on the platforms.

Highlights include Vito Acconci's *Wall-Slide* at 161st Street Yankee Stadium (above), Jeff Chien-Hsing Liao's light box panorama (42nd Street Bryant Park), illustrations of buskers within cars by R Gregory Christie and Roy Lichtenstein's *Times Square Mural*. When the first phase of the Second Avenue line opens in late 2016, look for new pieces by Sarah Sze, Chuck Close and Jean Shin. *www.mta.info/art*

Studio Museum in Harlem

Devoted primarily to the work of artists of African descent, the Studio Museum began life in 1968 in a rented loft and moved here in 1979. Under the leadership of Thelma Golden, and renovated and expanded by architects Rogers Marvel, the institution maintains its original mission of offering residencies to emerging artists (hence the 'Studio' in its name). Among those it has supported are Chakaia Booker, David Hammons, Kerry James Marshall and Julie Mehretu. There are now more than 2,000 works in the collection, which dates back to the 19th century, as well as the archive of Harlem Renaissance photographer James VanDerZee. 'Skin and Bones, 20 Years of Drawing' (above) celebrated two decades of work by Trenton Doyle Hancock.
144 W 125th Street, T 212 864 4500, www.studiomuseum.org

Paul Kasmin Gallery

This gallery opened in Soho in 1989 and moved to Chelsea a decade later following the northern migration of Manhattan's art scene. It now resides in a cluster of nearby properties at 293 and 297 Tenth Avenue and 515 W 27th Street, all of which host different rotating exhibitions. Represented are internationally recognised names such as Caio Fonseca ('New Paintings', above), Deborah Kass, Walton Ford, Nir Hod and Mark Ryden, and estate artists including Constantin Brâncuşi and William N Copley. The PK Shop, also at 297 Tenth Avenue, carries prints, jewellery, accessories and some great gifts: Kenny Scharf pool toys, Ron Arad's sinuous 'PizzaKobra' lamp, Roy Lichtenstein multiples and Anish Kapoor cufflinks. Closed Sunday and Monday. *297 Tenth Avenue, T 212 563 4474, www.paulkasmingallery.com*

BDDW

Carpenter, ceramicist and furniture-maker Tyler Hays' design studio is best known for its traditionally joined domestic hardwood pieces. Shaker-inspired tables, chairs, beds and mirrors are made by hand in Hays' Philadelphia atelier from natural materials including stone and clay, and the prices match the bespoke treatment. Ceramic mugs can fetch up to $500 each, but are still immediately snapped up. We were most taken by the 'Leaf' side table (above), $7,800, which is available in walnut, white oak or maple, and in natural oil or lacquer finish, as well as the dual-use ping-pong/dining table with leather net. The stylish 650 sq m BDDW emporium in Soho is airy and welcoming, with whitewashed arches, dark floors and a massive central skylight. *5 Crosby Street, T 212 625 1230, www.bddw.com*

Patrick Parrish

Since 1994, when he founded the Mondo Cane gallery, and later its popular spin-off blog, Patrick Parrish has been championing emerging artists and designers, many of whom he has given their first show in New York, and inspiring budding collectors. Within his eponymous Tribeca space, which feels more like an arts club than a shop, he displays an eclectic selection of midcentury furniture, lighting and decorative pieces,

such as Jim Walrod's collection of 1960s and 1970s Italian lamps (above), alongside pieces by the likes of Hanna Eshel, Emmett Moore, Doug Johnston and Jonathan Nesci. Visitors are encouraged to leaf through Parrish's many books, which are displayed on shelves created by RO/LU studio, as was the communal desk. Closed Sunday. *50 Lispenard Street, T 212 219 9244, www.patrickparrish.com*

SculptureCenter

Founded back in 1928 as The Clay Club and renamed in the 1940s, SculptureCenter's current home, a former trolley repair shop, was redesigned by Maya Lin in 2001, and then expanded and given a new courtyard by local architect Andrew Berman in 2014. Under curator Mary Ceruti, the non-profit mini museum continues to raise awareness of important artists including Gedi Sibony, Seth Price and Monika Sosnowska. Recent shows have featured the Brazilian Erika Verzutti and the Detroit sculptor/video artist Michael E Smith, while the 'Puddle, Porthole, Portal' exhibition showcased new work by Chadwick Rantanen (*Well*, above) and also brought Keiichi Tanaami's sculptures to the United States for the first time. Closed Tuesday and Wednesday.
*44-19 Purves Street, Long Island City,
T 718 361 1750, www.sculpture-center.org*

Eleven Rivington

Mainly highlighting young New York-based artists, Eleven Rivington opened in 2007 in the Lower East Side and its success led to expansion into a second, larger premises around the corner five years later. Next to Lehmann Maupin's downtown gallery (T 212 254 0054), the newer site is located in a creative hub where the band Talking Heads and fashion brand Odin were once based, accessed through a stone arch.

Architects Slade designed the stark white spaces. Among the talent represented here are Chris Caccamise, Jacob Kassay, Mary Heilmann, Michael DeLucia, Berliner Volker Hueller, Brazilian Caetano de Almeida and Icelander Katrín Sigurdardóttir, whose installations ('Ellefu', above) play with scale to question perceptions of urban space.
11 Rivington Street and 195 Chrystie Street, T 212 982 1930, www.elevenrivington.com

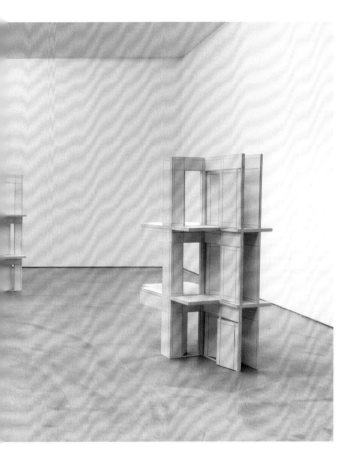

Cooper Hewitt

Founded in 1896, the Cooper Hewitt came under the stewardship of the Smithsonian in 1968 and soon moved into the Georgian-style mansion that was Andrew Carnegie's former home. After a $91m renovation by Gluckman Mayner, it reopened in 2014 as a newly interactive venture that brings the national design museum into the present day – digital pens enable you to collate and curate information, or you can create and project your own wallpaper. There is now more room for rotating shows, such as the 'Selects' series in the Marks Gallery (above), as well as the widely regarded permanent collection, which is exhaustive, from Milton Glaser's poster of Bob Dylan to Olivetti's 'Valentine' typewriter, Eames chairs and textiles from around the world. *2 E 91st Street, T 212 849 8400, www.cooperhewitt.org*

Park Avenue Armory

Many of the sons of New York's wealthiest families served in the Seventh Regiment of the National Guard, and its Park Avenue Armory HQ, designed by Charles Clinton in the Gothic revival style and opened in 1881, was the setting of glitzy social events among interiors by Tiffany and Stanford White. Since 2007, it has hosted large-scale productions of visual and performing arts, from Shakespeare plays to the New York Philharmonic and even a carnival with a full-size Ferris wheel, in the 5,100 sq m Wade Thompson Drill Hall (above), which is a triumph of iron-frame construction and one of the largest unobstructed interiors in the city. The ongoing $200m restoration by Herzog & de Meuron will bring, among other treats, a new copper mansard roof. *643 Park Avenue, T 212 616 3930, www.armoryonpark.org*

Noguchi Museum
In 1960, the Japanese-American artist
Isamu Noguchi set up a studio and home
in Queens that evolved into this museum.
Here you can see all manner of his work,
including his elemental sculptures; set
designs for Martha Graham; and papery
Akari lamps. The garden of weeping
cherry trees and bamboo is delightful.
9-01 33rd Road, Long Island City,
T 718 204 7088, www.noguchi.org

ARCHITOUR

A GUIDE TO NEW YORK'S ICONIC BUILDINGS

Chicago is the birthplace of the skyscraper, Dubai claims the tallest structure in the world, and Shanghai has more towers, but no city is as closely identified with the high-rise as New York. Money was the motivation to reach for the sky, but symbolism has always been immensely important here, from the automotive fantasies of Van Alen's art deco Chrysler Building (405 Lexington Avenue) to the defiant reach of One WTC (see p009). Indeed, it may be Gothamites' inordinate love of height that has enabled the city centre to retain its vibrancy, while so many US conurbations have become victims of suburban sprawl. It keeps on rising too, thanks to interventions including 432 Park Avenue (see p014), Christian de Portzamparc's One57, home to the Park Hyatt (see p016), Frank Gehry's 8 Spruce Street and Herzog & de Meuron's 56 Leonard (56 Leonard Street), a 250m jumble of condos that resembles a shiny Jenga stack.

There's also much new to see without craning your neck. Bjarke Ingels' tetrahedron-shaped 625 West 57th Street evokes a pyramid: 'The lovechild of a courtyard building and a skyscraper,' he has said. The old Hudson Yards rail depot regeneration project is eagerly awaited and, nearby, the Whitney Museum (see p074) has moved in to the Meatpacking District. Its former address, the 1966 Breuer Building (945 Madison Avenue) is now a contemporary wing of the Metropolitan Museum of Art (1000 Fifth Avenue, T 212 535 7710). *For full addresses, see Resources.*

New Museum

It isn't often that an art space has much in common with a rubbish bin. In actual fact, SANAA's New Museum of Contemporary Art, launched in 2007, may be the only building to be clad in the same aluminium wire mesh as its city's trash receptacles. When the design – a series of piled-up silvery boxes – was revealed in 2003, it looked delightful yet impossible (not to mention improbable, given its location

on historically unsavoury Bowery). New York changes fast, though, and what once seemed so alien (a fine-art museum on a street once known for homeless shelters) now makes sense. Enjoying its moment, the area is rife with swank restaurants and hip hotels, and in 2013, the Hester Street Café took up residence in the museum itself. *235 Bowery, T 212 219 1222, www.newmuseum.org*

Whitney Museum of American Art

Founded in 1930 by Eleanor Vanderbilt Whitney, this iconic museum's cutting-edge 22,000-piece art collection was always way cooler than its Upper East Side residency. That changed in 2015 with the opening of this 20,400 sq m home designed by Renzo Piano. Anchoring the south of the High Line (see p030), the Whitney's asymmetrical form draws on the Meatpacking District's industrial character, utilising concrete, steel and low-iron glass, and provides some of the largest display spaces found in the city. Flit between the eight storeys, outdoor landings, one of which opened with Mary Heilmann's playful *Sunset* installation, and ground-floor restaurant, where Michael Anthony cooks up superb US fare, using Richard Artschwager's funky elevators. *99 Gansevoort Street, T 212 570 3600, www.whitney.org*

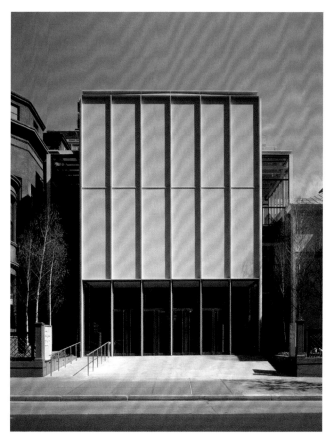

The Morgan Library & Museum

Since JP Morgan Jr donated his father's personal library to the people of New York in 1924, it has to be said that not many of the great unwashed have felt the need to venture in. The collection of Gutenberg Bibles, manuscripts and paintings has always given off enough of an elitist whiff to scare the masses away. Renzo Piano's sublime 2006 expansion added an entrance on Madison Avenue, a glazed atrium and several galleries, increasing the exhibition space by more than 50 per cent – a design intended to beckon people in and pull together the three existing buildings. The Morgan has now become a destination museum and host to swanky, and lucrative, soirées. The old robber baron would have been pleased.
225 Madison Avenue, T 212 685 0008, www.themorgan.org

Austrian Cultural Forum

In a city where bigger is regularly thought to be better, Austrian Raimund Abraham created a diminutive wonder in 2002 with his first major US project, although he had lived in New York for more than 30 years. 'My intention was to resolve the extreme condition of the smallness of the site,' he said. The architect, who passed in 2010, succeeded. The Cultural Forum is a brilliant design: a glass-skinned sliver, a mere 7.6m wide, rising to 85m. Its presence belies its dimensions, and the ACFNY's brooding facade – reminiscent, in profile, of an Easter Island statue – outshines all the surrounding buildings. When it was unveiled, it was hailed by many as the most important structure to have been erected in Manhattan in four decades.
11 E 52nd Street, T 212 319 5300,
www.acfny.org

Seagram Building

Mies van der Rohe's 1958 masterpiece typified his less-is-more philosophy and is a triumph of the International Style. In fact, he stated this was his only work in the US that met his stringent European standards of design, borrowed from the architect's classic German Pavilion built for the 1929 Barcelona World Expo. It was the first tower to use floor-to-ceiling windows to achieve the modernist ideal of a curtain of glass, and although American construction codes prevented him from displaying the structural steel frame, Mies added non-supportive bronze-tinted beams. Despite the austere aesthetic, the extravagant use of materials meant this was the world's most expensive building at the time. It served as a model for almost every NYC skyscraper that followed.
375 Park Avenue, www.375parkavenue.com

FDR Four Freedoms Park

Louis Kahn was commissioned to create a memorial to FDR on Roosevelt Island in 1973. Working with landscape architect Harriet Pattison, Kahn conceived a simple design based on two quintessential forms: the room and the garden. He shaped a 'room' from large granite blocks, forming a serene space on the tip of the island. An extract from FDR's 1941 'Four Freedoms' speech is carved on one wall, opposite a 1933 bronze bust of the former president by sculptor Jo Davidson. Two paths lined with linden trees edge the triangular lawn. Kahn's death in 1974 and economic hitches delayed construction until 2010, and the park finally opened in 2012. Set between Queens and Manhattan, it's a stunning site, accessible by cable car. Closed Tuesday.
Roosevelt Island, T 212 204 8831, www.fdrfourfreedomspark.org

SHOPS

THE BEST RETAIL THERAPY AND WHAT TO BUY

New York offers an abundance of seductive stores, from the glossy boutiques that line Madison Avenue to the niche outlets that dot Brooklyn. RePOP (see po92), The Future Perfect (55 Great Jones Street, T 212 473 2500), R & Company (82 Franklin Street, T 212 343 7979) and BDDW (see po63) set the bar high for design, and the thoughtful selection of homewares at The Primary Essentials (see po90) packs a punch. Also hugely diverting is the store helmed by the renowned vintage and antiques collector Paula Rubenstein (21 Bond Street, T 212 966 8954), an airy Noho space full of Navajo textiles, folk art, furniture and industrial objects.

The 2013 launch of Dover Street Market (160 Lexington Avenue, T 646 837 7750) brought energy to Murray Hill; as at the original venture in London, it carries edgy, lesser-known labels alongside exclusive collaborations with the likes of Prada and Calvin Klein. Soho never goes out of style, and additions such as denim den 3x1 (opposite) and the eco-friendly shoe designer Feit (see po89) on nearby Bowery sweeten the pot. Cobbled Crosby Street continues to strengthen its reputation for covetable retail. Check out eyewear designer Mykita (No 109, T 212 343 9100), cult menswear brand Carson Street Clothiers (No 63, T 212 925 2627) and the inaugural boutiques of lauded fashion designer Rachel Comey (No 95, T 212 334 0455), who opened here in 2014, and Miansai (see po95). *For full addresses, see Resources.*

LIGHT			MID			HEAVY			NOVELTY	
7	8	9	10	11	12	13	14	15	16	18

3x1

Scott Morrison, the impresario responsible for Paper Denim & Cloth and Earnest Sewn, is elevating the jean to new heights in this 370 sq m loft space. The name 3x1 comes from denim's weaving construction – and here you can order a bespoke pair of jeans tailored entirely to your own specifications. Choose from more than 250 varieties of selvedge denim woven on shuttle looms and sourced from mills around the world, many displayed on spools and available in a wide selection of colours and weights, before deciding on details such as stitching and adding hand-painted enamel buttons or custom-made zippers. Then, within two glass-enclosed ateliers in the middle of the room, your jeans are made to order. There is also a fine range of limited-edition styles, *15 Mercer Street, T 212 391 6969, www.3x1.us*

David Weeks Studio
Best known for his lighting as well as the
beloved wooden Cubebots, David Weeks
produces much more, as is evident on
a visit to his loft-like Tribeca showroom.
His creations include angular sofas, vivid
rugs and pliable animal figures, which
are displayed alongside collaborations
with artists such as Todd St John. It is
best to make an appointment.
38 Walker Street, T 212 966 3433

Proenza Schouler

Back in 2012, Jack McCollough and Lazaro Hernandez took their downtown style, so adored by art and fashion folk, uptown, to their first standalone space. To carve out a suitably directional emporium among Madison Avenue's swanky storefronts, the couple enlisted their friend, Brit architect David Adjaye, who had previously created their Soho office. The two-level townhouse interior, a mixture of glass, cement, wood and steel, has a minimal aesthetic, which enables Proenza Schouler's distinctive designs to shine. Adjaye then worked a similar magic on the brand's flagship in Soho (T 212 420 7300). Another duplex, this larger shop presents its womenswear and accessories against marble walls and on poured-concrete pedestals.
822 Madison Avenue, T 212 585 3200, www.proenzaschouler.com

Maryam Nassir Zadeh

This meticulously crafted boutique has been a favourite of fashion-forward New Yorkers since it opened in 2008. It is also known by its acronym MNZ, the initials of the Iranian-born, California-raised owner, who pools her inspiration from around the world – particularly Mexico, India and Paris – hence the bright colours that liven up the otherwise spare whitewashed brick and smooth concrete. You'll find pieces by established designers such as Marni and Acne Studios, lesser-known labels including Rosa Mosa (bags) and Castaner (shoes), as well as Zadeh's own tailored yet casual creations. Staples include breezy linen dresses and wide-leg cashmere trousers, accessorised with printed silk scarves, soft leather bags and whimsical felt hats. *123 Norfolk Street, T 212 673 6405, www.mnzstore.com*

Owen
Young retailer Phillip Salem is holding his own in the saturated Meatpacking District with his cult women's and men's boutique, opened in 2012 in a former florist. The cool mix of contemporary and emerging designers is perfectly matched by Jeremy Barbour's interior concept – 25,000 brown paper sacks near flawlessly stapled to the walls.
809 Washington Street, T 212 524 9770

Cadet

This crisp Brooklyn boutique, which has an interior punctuated with ammunition belts, vintage globes and a portrait of a Civil War general, reinforces the military-inspired look for which menswear label Cadet has gained street cred. Although owners Raul Arevalo and Brad Schmidt appreciate the precise lines and timeless appeal of historic uniforms, they apply a modern spin to their clothes. Wardrobe basics such as button-down shirts and slim trousers are the most popular pieces, and customers take full advantage of the free alteration service. Everything is made at Cadet's Bushwick factory and sold only in its own stores; there are further outposts in the East Village (T 646 633 4560) and Meatpacking District (T 917 722 2390). *46 N 6th Street, T 718 715 1695, www.cadetusa.com*

Feit

Founded by Australian brothers Tull and Josh Price, this neo-luxury footwear and accessories brand's minimalist aesthetic puts emphasis on method and technique (everything is handmade and hand-sewn), the use of only quality components – think vegetable-dyed Italian leather – and small-batch production. The store on the corner of Bowery, dreamt up in collaboration with the artist Jordana Maisie, features natural materials like Baltic birch and is billed as an installation rather than a traditional retail experience; and indeed, if you so desire, you can watch shoes such as the 'Hand Sewn High' sneakers (above), $520, being cobbled in the adjoining studio. Also on sale are leather goods, including belts, iPad cases and a range of wallets.
2 Prince Street, T 212 226 8600,
www.feitdirect.com

The Primary Essentials

An oasis of calm in the thick of Atlantic Avenue in Boerum Hill, Lauren Snyder's Brooklyn boutique sells design objects and artisanal curios from across the globe. The former fashion stylist selects items that she feels marry style and function. You may spy Nambu Tekki ironware, Helen Levi's artful ceramics and Earth Tu Face's natural skincare products. Snyder worked with her partner, architect Keith Burns, to customise the shop's interior, which is airy and uncluttered. Furnishings have been kept to a minimum: a blue marble counter and wooden display tables and cupboards. Keep an eye open for special commissions, including cord baskets by Doug Johnston and cotton bedwear by Sleepy Jones, which comes in a classic 'painted' blue stripe. *372 Atlantic Avenue, T 718 522 1804, www.theprimaryessentials.com*

Creatures of Comfort

It's difficult to believe that Creatures of Comfort has been holding court in Nolita since 2010: the vitality that it brought to this popular shopping area is still palpable. An eclectic mix of products is presented across the sprawling 230 sq m exposed-brick store, overseen by buyer and owner Jade Lai, who started the company in Los Angeles in 2005. Lai lures customers with goods spanning Japanese homewares to Bernhard Willhelm nail varnish. Best of all, though, is the fashion offering, specifically the womenswear. Creatures of Comfort's own ready-to-wear label is complemented by Lemaire, Band of Outsiders and Isabel Marant, among others. You'll also find a project space located in the shop, which hosts pop ups, exhibitions and events. *205 Mulberry Street, T 212 925 1005, www.creaturesofcomfort.us*

RePOP

It didn't take long for vintage-design purveyor RePOP to outgrow its original store in Brooklyn's Clinton Hill. To meet the surge in demand for his wares, which he sources from across the US, owner Russell Boyle moved to a larger location in Williamsburg in 2012, a 148 sq m space within the same building as the Roebling Tea Room (T 718 963 0760). The showroom brims with items from various eras, and makes for inspiring browsing as a result. It's worth spending at least an hour or so here so you can scour the stock properly. Covetable finds on our visit ranged from antique dress dummies to original Danish Modern dressers and one-off lighting fixtures. RePOP's prices are fairer than you'll find in Manhattan, and bargaining isn't ruled out. Boyle also offers personal design consultations by appointment.
143 Roebling Street, T 718 260 8032, www.repopny.com

Alexander Wang

A luxe but relaxed aesthetic has rendered Alexander Wang's womenswear a fashion-pack staple. Opened in 2011 on Soho's grungy-glam Grand Street, the brand's Ryan Korban-conceived main showroom is a blend of boutique, gallery and design den. The expansive all-white space boasts high ceilings, marble floors and a steel cage that is used for seasonal installations. After browsing Wang's sexy, downtown-friendly clothing and accessories, head to the centre of the shop, where a lounge area beckons you to kick off your heels or, considering the environs, your Nikes. The leather sofa and brass table stacked with books and magazines should allay any retail fatigue, as will the fox-fur hammock: simple but sumptuous, à la Wang.
103 Grand Street, T 212 977 9683,
www.alexanderwang.com

Miansai

Miami accessory brand Miansai, which launched with a single bracelet in 2008, opened this standalone flagship store in Soho just five years later and it has quickly carved a niche. Within a narrow, sleek, minimalist boutique with exposed brick, Italian ceramic tiling and wrought-iron window frames, you'll find a growing line of jewellery, leather goods and lifestyle accessories – lovely bound notebooks, wallets, watches and stylish two-tone bags – that have expanded the clientele base from intrinsically male to unisex. We remain fans of the signature brass anchor bracelet made with rope, $55, or leather, $65. A café counter at the front offers a variety of loose tea blends and kombucha, an obsession of founder Michael Saiger. *33 Crosby Street, T 212 858 9710, www.miansai.com*

ESCAPES

WHERE TO GO IF YOU WANT TO LEAVE TOWN

Gothamites claim that when you leave New York, you ain't going nowhere – although in summer, the city's border seems to stretch to include the length of Long Island. When the going gets hot, the hot crowd gets going (if you can stand the humidity in town, your reward will be blissfully empty shops and restaurants). Escape options are many, whether your taste is for an art expedition (see p098), surfing off Montauk – stay at The Surf Lodge (183 Edgemere Street, T 631 483 5037) or Ruschmeyer's (161 Second House Road, T 631 668 2877) – or hiking in the Catskills. Upstate, the cheekily named Stickett Inn (3380 Route 97, Barryville, T 845 557 0913) offers four modern suites and a log cabin. Situated by the scenic Delaware River, it's a two-hour drive from the city.

If you visit the Hamptons, make sure you have a friend with a house, or rent a place far in advance. To avoid bumper-to-bumper traffic, get there on the Cannonball train on the Long Island Rail Road, or the Hampton Jitney (www.hamptonjitney.com), whose glamorous passengers give new meaning to coach travel. Shelter Island is less intense; go by ferry and stay at André Balazs' Sunset Beach hotel (35 Shore Road, T 631 749 2001). Closer to the city, book one of the 12 artist-designed rooms at Playland Motel (97-20 Rockaway Beach Boulevard, T 347 954 9063), a hip hotel with a lively bar, just a block away from the locals' surf spot of choice. *For full addresses, see Resources.*

Topping Rose House, Bridgehampton

Relaunched in its present guise in spring 2013, Simon Critchell and Bill Campbell's Topping Rose House manages to convey a sense of history while fully embracing contemporary design. The property was subject to a dramatic three-year overhaul that saw Roger Ferris + Partners carefully restore the original 1842 house and barn, and add a brand-new building and modern cottages (all of which cater for guests), as well as a spa and event space. Another major attraction is the hotel's top-notch restaurant, helmed by lauded chef Tom Colicchio. The seasonal American menu makes the most of locally grown produce, including vegetables, fruit and herbs that are harvested from the property's farm. *One Bridgehampton, Sag Harbor Turnpike, Bridgehampton, T 631 537 0870, www.toppingrosehouse.com*

Parrish Art Museum, Long Island

Artists have populated Long Island's East End since the late 19th century, when commuting from New York was made easier by an extension of the Long Island Rail Road. Notable figures have been drawn by the light and the beauty of the landscape, from Impressionist William Merritt Chase to abstract expressionists Jackson Pollock and Willem de Kooning. The Parrish Art Museum was founded in Southampton in 1898, by collector Samuel Longstreth Parrish. In 2012, it moved into a new building by Herzog & de Meuron. Modelled on a local artist's studio, and featuring a pair of striking overhangs, the sky-lit space has tripled the exhibition area for the permanent collection of early 19th-century to present-day East End art. *279 Montauk Highway, Water Mill, T 631 283 2118, www.parrishart.org*

Richard Meier Model Museum

If you're looking for a reason to venture over the Hudson, Richard Meier's Model Museum is an excellent one. Located in the Mana Contemporary art complex, it displays more than 400 handmade architectural models created during the architect's 50-year career. One of the most notable is an 11m-long model of the Getty Center in LA, made entirely from wood. An archive of small-scale sketches, photographs and renderings is exhibited across floor-to-ceiling shelves. Intended as a resource for both visitors and students, the museum also houses Meier's research library and displays some of his artwork. His daughter, Ana Meier, has a furniture showroom next door. Visits are by appointment only. *Mana Contemporary, 888 Newark Avenue, Jersey City*

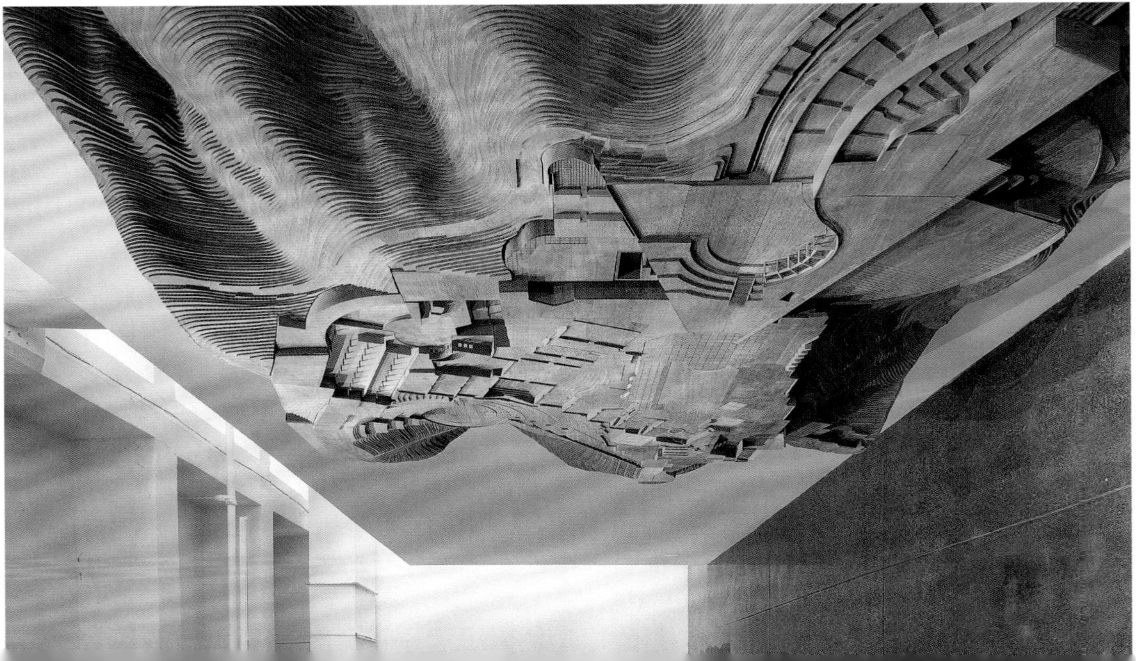

Glass House, New Canaan
The Connecticut town of New Canaan,
about 50 miles north-east of NYC, boasts
some of the finest examples of modern
American architecture. The most famous
is Philip Johnson's home, the Glass House
(pictured), completed in 1949. It is perhaps
the purest expression of the International
Style. Tours must be booked in advance.
Visitor Center, 199 Elm Street,
T 203 594 9884, www.theglasshouse.org

NOTES

SKETCHES AND MEMOS

RESOURCES

CITY GUIDE DIRECTORY

A

About Glamour 054
107a N 3rd Street
Brooklyn
T 718 599 3044
www.aboutglamour.strikingly.com

Alder 036
157 Second Avenue
T 212 539 1900
www.aldernyc.com

Aldo Sohm Wine Bar 052
151 W 51st Street
T 212 554 1143
www.aldosohmwinebar.com

Alexander Wang 094
103 Grand Street
T 212 977 9683
www.alexanderwang.com

All'onda 048
22 E 13th Street
T 212 231 2236
www.allondanyc.com

Almanac 032
28 Seventh Avenue S
T 212 255 1795
www.almanacnyc.com

Antica Pesa 050
115 Berry Street
Brooklyn
T 347 763 2635
www.anticapesa.com

The Apartment by The Line 026
3rd floor
76 Greene Street
T 646 678 4908
www.theline.com

Attaboy 024
134 Eldridge Street

AT&T Building 012
32 Sixth Avenue

Austrian Cultural Forum 076
11 E 52nd Street
T 212 319 5300
www.acfny.org

B

BDDW 063
5 Crosby Street
T 212 625 1230
www.bddw.com

Le Bernardin 052
155 W 51st Street
T 212 554 1515
www.le-bernardin.com

The Black Ant 032
60 Second Avenue
T 212 598 0300
www.theblackantnyc.com

Bossa Nova Civic Club 032
1271 Myrtle Avenue
Bushwick
T 718 443 1271
www.bossanovacivicclub.com

Breuer Building 072
945 Madison Avenue

C

Cadet 088
46 N 6th Street
Williamsburg
T 718 715 1695
305 E 9th Street
T 646 633 4560
69 Eighth Avenue
T 917 722 2390
www.cadetusa.com

Carson Street Clothiers 080
63 Crosby Street
T 212 925 2627
www.carsonstreetclothiers.com

HOTELS

ADDRESSES AND ROOM RATES

Archer 022
Room rates:
double, from $270;
Archer King, from $270
45 W 38th Street
T 212 719 4100
www.archerhotel.com/new-york

The Bowery House 044
Room rates:
double, from $130
220 Bowery
T 212 837 2373
www.theboweryhouse.com

Edition 016
Room rates:
double, from $725
5 Madison Avenue
T 212 413 4200
www.editionhotels.com

The High Line Hotel 016
Room rates:
double, from $400
180 Tenth Avenue
T 212 929 3888
www.thehighlinehotel.com

Hotel Hugo 016
Room rates:
double, from $420
525 Greenwich Street
T 212 608 4848
www.hotelhugony.com

Loews Regency 016
Room rates:
double, from $300
540 Park Avenue
T 212 759 4100
www.loewshotels.com/regency-hotel

The Ludlow 016
Room rates:
double, from $225
180 Ludlow Street
T 212 432 1818
www.theludlownyc.com

The Marlton 019
Room rates:
double, from $250;
Queen Deluxe, from $275
5 W 8th Street
T 212 321 0100
www.marltonhotel.com

The Marmara Park Avenue 023
Room rates:
double, from $550;
One Bedroom Suite, price on request
114 E 32nd Street
T 212 427 3100
park.marmaranyc.com

The NoMad Hotel 051
Room rates:
double, from $425
1170 Broadway
T 212 796 1500
www.thenomadhotel.com

1 Hotel Central Park 016
Room rates:
double, from $475
1414 Sixth Avenue
T 212 703 2001
www.1hotels.com

Paper Factory 018
Room rates:
double, from $170
37-06 36th Street
Long Island City
T 718 392 7200
www.paperfactoryhotel.com

Park Hyatt 016
Room rates:
double, from $800
153 W 57th Street
T 646 774 1234
www.newyork.park.hyatt.com

Playland Motel 096
Room rates:
double, from $100
97-20 Rockaway Beach Boulevard
Rockaway Beach
T 347 954 9063
www.playlandmotel.com

Ruschmeyer's 096
Room rates:
double, from $450
161 Second House Road
Montauk
Long Island
T 631 668 2877
www.chelseahotels.com

Sixty Soho 017
Room rates:
double, from $320
60 Thompson Street
T 877 431 0400
www.sixtyhotels.com

The Standard East Village 045
Room rates:
double, from $400
25 Cooper Square
T 212 475 5700
www.standardhotels.com/east-village

Stickett Inn 096
Room rates:
prices on request
3380 Route 97
Barryville
T 845 557 0913
www.stickettinn.com

Sunset Beach 096
Room rates:
double, from $480
35 Shore Road
Shelter Island Heights
Long Island
T 631 749 2001
www.sunsetbeachli.com

The Surf Lodge 096
Room rates:
double, from $400
183 Edgemere Street
Montauk
Long Island
T 631 483 5037
www.thesurflodge.com

Topping Rose House 097
Room rates:
double, from $525
One Bridgehampton
Sag Harbor Turnpike
Bridgehampton
Long Island
T 631 537 0870
www.toppingrosehouse.com

Viceroy 016
Room rates:
double, from $385
120 W 57th Street
T 212 830 8000
www.viceroyhotelsandresorts.com

Wythe Hotel 020
Room rates:
double, from $350;
King Room, from $450
80 Wythe Avenue
Brooklyn
T 718 460 8000
www.wythehotel.com

WALLPAPER* CITY GUIDES

Executive Editor
Jeremy Case

Author
Marie Elena Martinez

Art Editor
Eriko Shimazaki

Photography Editor
Elisa Merlo
Assistant Photography Editor
Nabil Butt

Sub-Editor
Belle Place

Editorial Assistant
Emilee Jane Tombs

Contributors
Katie Chang
David Kaufman
Pei-Ru Keh
Julie Lasky

Interns
Tolu Ogundipe
Killian Reimers

Production Controller
Sophie Kullmann

Wallpaper*® is a
registered trademark
of Time Inc (UK)

First published 2006
Revised and updated
2008, 2009, 2010, 2011,
2013 and 2014
Ninth edition 2015

© Phaidon Press Limited

All prices and venue
information are correct
at time of going to press,
but are subject to change.

Original Design
Loran Stosskopf
Map Illustrator
Russell Bell

Contacts
wcg@phaidon.com
@wallpaperguides

More City Guides
www.phaidon.com/travel

Phaidon Press Limited
Regent's Wharf
All Saints Street
London N1 9PA

Phaidon Press Inc
65 Bleecker Street
New York, NY 10012

Phaidon® is a registered
trademark of Phaidon
Press Limited

www.phaidon.com

A CIP Catalogue record for
this book is available from
the British Library.

Printed in China

ISBN 978 0 7148 7035 9

PHOTOGRAPHERS

Iwan Baan
High Line, p030

Ron Blunt
Glass House, pp102-103

Roger Casas
Hearst Tower, p013
Woolworth Building, p015
Austrian Cultural
Forum, p076
Seagram Building, p077

Elizabeth Felicella
Noguchi Museum,
pp070-071

Baldomero Fernandez
Creatures of Comfort, p091

**Judd Foundation/VAGA,
NY/DACS**
101 Spring Street,
p028, p029

Dean Kaufman
New Museum, p073

Michael Moran
SculptureCenter, p065

Fran Parente
New York city view,
inside front cover

9/11 Memorial, pp010-011
432 Park Avenue, p014
Sixty Soho, p017
Paper Factory, p018
The Marlton, p019
Archer, p022
The Marmara Park Avenue,
p023
The Apartment by
The Line, pp026-027
Eleven Madison Park, p031
Russ & Daughters
Cafe, p033
Lois, p034, p035
Up & Down, p038
Momofuku Ko, p039
Dirt Candy, p040
Tørst, p041
Cosme, pp042-043
Pearl & Ash, p044
Narcissa, p045
Toro, p046
Chefs Club, p047
All'onda, pp048-049
Antica Pesa, p050
NoMad Bar, p051
Aldo Sohm Wine Bar, p052
The Cecil, p053
Nadia Sarwar, p055
Chamber, p057
MTA Arts & Design, p060
Paul Kasmin Gallery, p062
Patrick Parrish, p064
Whitney Museum of
American Art, p074
3x1, p081

David Weeks
Studio, pp082-083
Proenza Schouler, p084
Maryam Nassir Zadeh,
p085
Cadet, p088
The Primary
Essentials, p090
RePOP, pp092-093
Miansai, p095

Peartree Digital
Feit, p089

Matthu Placek
Parrish Art Museum,
pp098-099

Andrew Romer
Pioneer Works, pp058-059

Mark Rose
Topping Rose House, p097

Jason Schmidt
David Zwirner, p025

Steven Sze
Richard Meier Model
Museum, pp100-101

Paul Warchol
FDR Four Freedoms
Park, pp078-079

NEW YORK
A COLOUR-CODED GUIDE TO THE HOT 'HOODS

TRIBECA/THE BATTERY
Lower Manhattan embraces Wall Street and, to the north, hip retail and restaurants

UPPER WEST SIDE
This is Woody Allen territory, characterised by the apartment blocks of the bourgeoisie

WEST VILLAGE
A charming district full of tree-lined avenues, and plenty of chichi boutiques and cafés

SOHO
Big fashion brands attract tourists, but there are interesting galleries in the area too

UPPER EAST SIDE
Visit the swanky stores on Madison Avenue and some of the best museums in the world

MIDTOWN
The throbbing business heart of New York is the location of the neon-tastic Times Square

CHELSEA
New York's power art crowd gather day and night in this slick West Side neighbourhood

EAST VILLAGE/LOWER EAST SIDE
Cool bars, shops and cultural spaces pepper this increasingly wealthy part of town

For a full description of each neighbourhood, see the Introduction.
Featured venues are colour-coded, according to the district in which they are located.